CONTENTS

Introduction

Part 1 – THE LOSS

   Session 1 – Letting go what life has taken   4
   Session 2 – Letting go what life has failed to give   6

Part 2 – THE CALL

   Session 3 – Letting go our possessions, security and control   9
   Session 4 – Letting go our conditioning and others' expectations   13
   Session 5 – Letting go life denying attitudes, feelings, thoughts   18
   Session 6 – Letting go our past and ourselves   22

Appendices

   A – Guided Meditation on letting go   26
   B – Guided Meditation on loss   27
   C – Guided Meditation on the past and guilt   28

Book List   29

Guidelines for Group Leaders   30

INTRODUCTION

THE THEME

Western culture lays great stress on activity, effort and achievement. We view with suspicion any passivity, any lack of control. This attitude has also extended to our spirituality. Much of our spiritual 'work' has entailed striving, climbing into the light, improving our souls, effort, struggle, mental fight, will power and self-control. We have neglected the other way: of letting *'the dark come upon you which shall be the darkness of God'* (T S Eliot), the way of sinking, letting things happen in our psyche, relaxing and waiting on God. Letting go and letting God . . .

Some mystics have known the need for this inner letting go, by which we make room for God's activity in us. Meister Eckhart speaks of the cessation of mental, emotional and physical activity as preparing ourselves so that God can work on our transformation and the birth of God in us.

In this state of just being before God, when we cease to divide ourselves into good and evil, cease to struggle against that in us of which we disapprove, we can be receptive and pliable. We may even be able to sing with Charles Wesley, *'Mould as thou wilt thy passive clay'* and mean it!

This course has been designed to help us to grow as people and as Christians, through letting go of, dying to, that which diminishes us.

THE METHOD

In each session we will attempt:

> to see and accept our need for letting go in different areas.

> to let the Holy Spirit enable us to do it – through exploring what the Bible has to say and through sharing and prayer.

SHARING is the most important part of each session. To make this possible the following points should be considered:

1. Everyone's experience is valid and must not be put into question.
2. It is a great privilege to listen to another's personal sharing and it must be done with respect and gentleness.
3. Each person must be allowed to share uninterrupted.
4. It is right to show emotions and to cry.
5. There is no need to hurry to the 'rescue' of those who do.
6. No-one must be pressed to share if they would rather not.
7. Everything said within the group is confidential to the group.

SUGGESTIONS

There may be more material in this study than you are able to use during your time together. The study has been left flexible in the hope that you will be led to your greatest need and can choose what to deal with first.

For example, in Study 5 you could start with the theme of fear rather than that of self-contempt if that seems right. It is better to study one part thoroughly than to simply read or skim through the whole. The rest of the material can be used by individuals at home.

At the end of the study are some guided meditations (Appendices A, B and C) which can be used by the group at the end of the sessions if desired. They should be read very slowly with pauses of 20 seconds at the dots . . ., or they could be recorded on tape and played back, so that the whole group can take part.

Unless otherwise stated all scripture quotations are from the New Revised Standard Version.

My grateful thanks to Mary Austin, Palma Coggins, Emily Sherwood and Ivor Smith-Cameron for reading the typescript and for their most helpful comments. I am most grateful to Mary for also re-typing it on her word processor. My special thanks to Peter Wright for his drawing of the letting go hands.

PART 1 – THE LOSS

SESSION 1
LETTING GO WHAT LIFE HAS TAKEN

Everybody knows loss. We have all suffered at least one serious loss: by being born we lost the safety and security, the dark, warm and pulsating environment of our mother's womb. And throughout our lives at times of anxiety, stress and anguish, we tend to take up the foetal position and even rock. In these situations we still hanker after our pre-natal bliss.

From then on our losses are innumerable. Indeed, every change in life brings with it a loss of the old and familiar, even loved thing or person. Every choice we make implies loss of that which is not chosen. We could make a long list of our losses including, for many, unemployment, repossession of home, bereavement, disability through accident or illness and many others.

J. Neville Ward says in his book, *Friday Afternoon*:

> *All suffering is change that is felt to be simply loss – of someone or something considered necessary to life, and so loss that is resented and rejected. The work of suffering involves drawing on one's inner resources to find the ability to let go what life has taken to accept the change made by its absence, and to achieve a new position from which life continues to be possible. The result of this work is the growth of the spirit, which we believe is a large amount of what living is for.*

We deal with loss through grief, and there is no loss without grief. Unfortunately, our culture doesn't allow the expression of such grief but its suppression makes the process of letting go more difficult.

Turkish proverb *The person who conceals grief finds no relief from it.*

SHARE

What do you think of the old adage, 'Boys don't cry'?

Is there an equivalent for women?

When my husband died, some of my friends must have been so afraid that I might show grief that every time I mentioned him they would change the subject.

Have you ever encouraged anyone to weep? Should we?

READ *John 11:32-35* *Story of Lazarus. Asked out of compassion*

Sooner or later all of us will know the pain of bereavement, whether by death, divorce, separation or betrayal, or loss of work. However deep and painful the wound, the quality of our continuing life and the lives of those around us will depend on whether we choose to let go the person or thing lost and so choose life, or cling to the past and diminish ourselves and others. **Therefore choose life!** *We can't do this straight away but during the grieving process it must start to happen*

I remember a great aunt of mine whose only daughter died young. For the rest of her long life she refused to accept her loss, to let the girl go. As a child I pitied her long-suffering husband. Laughter was banned from their home – they had to continue in mourning. The fact that he was still there seemed to go unnoticed.

READ *2 Samuel 18:31-19:8*

SHARE

How was David helped to let go of Absalom? *Joab reminds David of his love of others + reminds him.*

How can we help people in similar situations?

What might have made David's letting go of his son more difficult? *Because of his betrayal*

Can it be that letting go of an unsatisfactory relationship, which is unresolved, presents a more complex difficulty?

Do you think one can complete the unfinished business of a difficult or unsatisfactory relationship after the death of the other person?

How might this be done?

Would writing a letter, writing an imaginary answer from the deceased, writing again – communicating with that person in your imagination – help? Many say that it does. (NB Not spiritualist seances!)

PRAYER

God, our Father,
Help us when the hour of loss and grief has come, to face the suffering it brings with courage and patience. Help us, also, not to cling but to let go what we have lost and to move on, trusting the promise of a fuller life which can grow out of the death of the old.

Disappointments

SESSION 2
LETTING GO WHAT LIFE HAS FAILED TO GIVE

Our losses consist not only of what 'life has taken' but also of what life has failed to give.

Most of us grow up with certain expectations. *Any others?* They may include any of these: to get a good education, a job, a certain standard of living, to get married and have children. We expect our marriage to be happy, our children to bring us much happiness and to help us when we are old; we expect to have freedom to choose, the house to make our home in, our friends, holidays . . . the list is endless.

For various reasons many of these expectations may remain unfulfilled. A friend of mine used to introduce herself by giving her name and adding, 'Miss, not by choice'. She belonged to the generation in which many women remained unmarried because so many young men did not return from the war.

But choices are very rare now. Many opt for independence.

Being single may be a God-given opportunity to cultivate being alone, to think and to meditate, to be creative, to enjoy and learn from nature. The Church has often prevented these possibilities by considering single people the proper 'material' to fill the many Church offices and jobs. And many married people look back with nostalgia on the freedom of being single.

One hears of couples pursuing a determined, costly struggle to have a child which sometimes ends in disappointment.

Most children can expect to grow up in a happy enough home, but an increasing number experience the break up of their homes after maybe years of tensions and fights; some are treated cruelly, some only know one parent and may miss the other one throughout life. Some, due to a mental handicap, may be brought up in an institution, far from their families.

The freedom to choose, so much taken for granted in our society, is limited for many by being born into poverty, an unsatisfactory family situation, physical or mental disablement, or by society's race discrimination or other prejudices.

According to recent statistics, many citizens of our country of earning age are destined to remain unemployed, and as new technology takes over more and more of our jobs, the result may be an 'underclass' of people who lack the necessary skills and who are therefore unemployable.

Strain on those in work + expectation that people will ever more than 1 job.

We may hope to die surrounded by a loving family but end up on a noisy ward of a large hospital, alone.

In many of these situations we may find it most difficult to let go, dreaming that life may still deliver to us what we feel we have a right to expect, and to concentrate on what we have and make the best of it is a very tall order indeed. But in all these situations there is still work to be done by the person affected by the disappointment and much can be done by those around them to satisfy at least some of their needs.

L'Arche is a movement started over twenty-five years ago which aims at providing a family substitute for people with a mental handicap who have spent their childhood and young adulthood in institutions. Here young volunteers live with the residents in small households, sharing chores and meals, playing and praying together. Amazing transformations can take place in some when they experience acceptance, and the value and support of such a 'family'. One man's witness was: *'In hospital they did not know the meaning of my life; here they know the meaning of my life.'* Needless to say not all are capable of change. Some have been wounded so deeply that they are withdrawn, unable to respond.

One of the greatest disappointments in life can involve one's children. So many hopes and emotions, so much hard work is invested in them. The saddest radio messages, I find, are the SOS ones: *'Would Tom, last seen twenty years ago, please contact St James' hospital where his father/mother is dangerously ill.'* A TV documentary showed a group of secondary schoolchildren offering help to housebound old people. A bedridden woman, unco-operative and unfriendly, cried out, 'I don't want your help! I have children, they should look after me!'

Jesus knew much disappointment in his life.

He invested most of his ministry in nurturing the little band of disciples, yet how disappointing they were.

> On the way to Jerusalem, when he spoke of his forthcoming suffering and death, Peter, with a complete lack of understanding, tried to dissuade him. *Mark 8:31-33*
>
> When he knew he was approaching his final test and Passion, James and John were planning how to get the highest places in his kingdom. *Mark 10:32-45*

In the Upper Room the disciples were still quarrelling about which of them was the greatest.
Luke:22:24

In Gethsemane Jesus longed to have his closest friends' prayerful support, but they fell asleep.
Luke 22:39-46

SHARE

How can we let go what we expect from life but do not get?

Consider these suggestions:

1. Face the situation honestly. Admit the truth and enter the reality of your pain, very much like a woman in childbirth must not resist the pain but relax into it. Only after we accept the reality of our pain can we let it go and arrive on the other side of it, able to acknowledge, welcome and appreciate what we still have and can enjoy.

2. Live a day at a time. This day can be good and enjoyable. Expect it to be. Concentrate on appreciating what you have today.

3. Cultivate faith in the goodness of life as given to us by our loving God whose Spirit is at work in us, transforming us and using our *every* experience to this end.

Is it possible to enjoy life in spite of a deep-seated ache of disappointment?

Can such an ache be healed?

How can we achieve the inner freedom to enjoy what we have rather than hanker after what we miss?

Please speak only from experience.

PRAYER

Take time to write a prayer of protest at your loss.

Write a prayer of grief at your loss.

If you can, share your prayer with the group.

Either alone or in groups of two or three write a 'let go' prayer.

In intercession remember all who suffer loss, the bereaved and those who cling to what they have lost. Think also of the work of L'Arche and organisations such as CRUSE, helping the widowed, and the Society of Compassionate Friends, specifically for bereaved parents.

PART 2 – THE CALL

In the next four sessions we are going to consider both the special call an individual may receive and the call every Christian receives; to develop into full humanity, to life, to freedom, to kingdom living.

READ
    Isaiah 55:1-3   Deuteronomy 30:15-20   Matthew 6:19-21, 24-34

At this call we must let go many things, only a few of which can be considered here.

SESSION 3
LETTING GO POSSESSIONS, SECURITY, CONTROL

Jesus did not need to be poor. As a carpenter he must have been moderately well off. He did not need to associate with the poor and those considered as outcasts. He was a member of an artisan family, no doubt a respected member of his village society. He left these comforts at the call of God to proclaim the coming kingdom and motivated by his compassion for the poor and the rejected. He abandoned the settled life of home and the security of work and became first a travelling preacher, then an outcast among outcasts, soon to be rejected and condemned.

    He calls us also to put the kingdom of God first:
to hold lightly to possessions	Matt. 6:24-34
to be generous and humble	Luke 6:27-36
to follow him whatever the outcome	Luke 9:57-62
Some found it too difficult and went away	Mark 10:17-27

SHARE

    Was it only wealth the rich man would have to give up?
    What else does wealth bring, apart from material advantages?
    Which are the most difficult to let go?

All of us have some power over others: in families, work places, in schools and in the church. But wealth brings much power with it and many opportunities to exercise it.

As part of a Lent course some years ago I saw a film about Christians in Korea. We saw a house group meeting composed entirely of millionaires and their wives and were shown the factory of one of the men. He claimed he looked after his work force well: through welfare projects and through religion. They all had to start every day by attending the chapel service.

> Do you consider that such exercise of power over others is justified by the good end it was meant to serve?
>
> If not, why not?
>
> Is having wealth an added temptation to exercise our tyrannical streak?

Our possessions are of many different kinds. We accumulate them: culture, educational achievements, promotions, status – in our society, Church and work place.

There is nothing intrinsically wrong with riches of any kind. However, they tend to so fill our lives that there is no room left for what really matters: that we love, that we grow, that we are open to the creative influence of God at work in us and that we live God's kingdom now.

> *There, where clinging to things ends*
> *is where God begins to be . . .*
> *if you wish to receive divine joy and God*
> *first pour out your clinging to things.*
>
> *Meditations with Meister Eckhart*, Matthew Fox

Some found it possible:

> St Francis, son of a wealthy merchant, let go his wealth, comforts and privileges in order to follow his Lord and 'lady poverty'. Had he remained in business we would never have heard of him.
>
> The unnamed little boy let go all he had: five loaves and two fishes and Jesus was able to feed five thousand. *John 6:5-13*
>
> The early Christians, enabled by the Holy Spirit, did surrender all and found new community, new life, new joy and peace.
> *Acts 2:43-47, 4:32-37*

This early Christian 'communism' did not last. As the Lord delayed his second coming and they had disposed of their capital they were soon in need. But even then they experienced in the love and generous caring of the Gentile Christians the new life of the kingdom.
2 Cor. 8:1-4

PRAYER
God of the poor, prune our lives of all that we cling to,
O Spirit of true wealth, draw us through the narrow gate of loss,
O Christ who lives in those we neglect, through their generosity
  turn us to repentance, that we may be forgiven.

Jim Cotter,
Through Desert Places

LETTING GO OUR CHILDREN

We often consider our children to be our most precious possessions. Yet throughout their lives we must gradually let them go.

I once attended a wedding where, after the father of the bride answered his question with, 'I do,' the mother of the bridegroom was also asked, 'Who gives this man in marriage?' and she too answered, 'I do.'

This transformed the ancient custom of the father renouncing his right to ownership and care of his daughter into a new one in which a deeper question was asked of both parents: letting go their children into new life independent of them. The old question became in reality: '*Do you release them to live their own lives according to their own decisions? Do you relinquish your demands and expectations?*'

How often parents are unable to do that. Their inability may result in strained or even broken relationships.

SHARE

Have you let your children go?

If they are still young how are you facing this prospect?

Share with the group how you find this possible.

Henri Nouwen speaks of our children as the most important guests in our homes, to whom we must give special attention, but who won't stay long, as they must follow their own way.

Is thinking of our children as our most important *guests* a helpful suggestion?

The story of the prodigal son (*Luke 15:11ff*) speaks of a father who let his son go twice. First he let go a son who rejected him and all his family stood for. The father accepted the rejection, the loss of property, and loss of prestige in his community, which would be very hard to bear in the Middle East. He swallowed his pride and let the boy go. But he was ready to welcome the son back the moment he appeared in view. Then he let him have the freedom of a reinstated son, freedom through forgiveness.

SESSION 4
LETTING GO OUR CONDITIONING

We are all conditioned, programmed from birth by:

>Our relatives.
>Our pre-school and school teachers.
>Youth organisations.
>TV . . . the Church . . .

That's how we become members of our family, class, society, nation, religion.

The story is told of a young IRA man serving a prison sentence. In his solitary cell he spent much time in prayer. He realised that his attitudes did not conform to those of the Gospel. He confided in the chaplain: 'I am praying to change, but I am hoping God won't answer that prayer. If he does, I would lose everything: my family, my background, my friends, my culture, even my conversation.' Only after God did answer his prayer did he realise that his gains were greater than his losses.

Jesus let go many of his culture's ideas and conditioning: what the Messiah ought to be, how women should be treated, what should be the relationship of men to women, and many others.

Jesus moved across the barriers of conditioning to encounter:

Lepers	*Luke 5:12-13*
Women: a Samaritan	*John 4:1-42*
one considered unclean	*Matt. 9:18-26*
Gentiles	*Luke 7:1-10*
Sinners	*Luke 19:1-10*

If we would follow him, we too must free ourselves from many of our cherished ideas, demands of our culture, prejudices and our need to conform. We have to unlearn a lot if we would live the life of God's kingdom. This unlearning can be so painful that it is like dying little deaths. But he who would keep his life, will lose it . . . Only Christ himself can accomplish this change of heart and mind, this *Metanoia* in us, if we prepare the ground.

Other disciples have had to do it before us:

>Peter would not allow Jesus to wash his feet – all his conditioning was against it. It was for a servant to wash his master's feet, not the

other way around. He had to let that conditioning go if he were to be a disciple of Jesus. *John 13:3-8*

Peter knew that a good Jew was not allowed to enter the house of a Gentile, certainly not to eat with him. It needed a vision for him to accept a new attitude. *Acts 10*

In silence consider your own conditioning for a few minutes.

Can you think of instances when you do not think your own thoughts but those of your father, mother, teacher, minister, friends, workmates?

Share in the group.

Together make a list of who and what conditioned you.

Divide it into positive and negative conditioning.

A cure depends on a good diagnosis.

In a couple of minutes of silence, decide which part of your conditioning does not belong to God's kingdom . . . Then try to let it go, maybe only some of it at first. Persist, and you may find that you gain a new freedom – from the bonds of conditioning.

If, instead of teaching people such narrow group solidarity and pride, we taught them how to understand what life is really like for others, and help them to release their painful memories and emotions, they might be able to think clearly in the search for common solutions.

SHARE

Are we, singly and as the Church trying, to do any of that?
Does the Church help us to let go our negative conditioning?

PRAYER

Pray for people whose lives are blighted by negative conditioning:
black and white in South Africa, Protestant and Catholic in Northern Ireland, Jews and Arabs in the Near East, Serbs, Croats and Bosnians in the Balkans. In our own country – ?

Pray for all who are engaged in trying to overcome such conditioning:
> The Corrymeela community in Northern Ireland and their recent outreach in Sri Lanka, also torn by the conflict caused by group conditioning.
> The work of the different Peace Studies Departments of Universities.
> Others known to you involved in similar activity.

LETTING GO OTHERS' EXPECTATIONS OF US

All of us must one day leave home and the bonds of family. We have to refuse to subject ourselves to the pressures put upon us, and not allow ourselves to become victims, living lives imposed on us by others.

We must choose freedom.

SHARE

> Is such an attitude to our families selfish?
>
> What do you think of the following statement? *Selfishness is not when you live your own life, but when you expect others to live according to your wishes?*

Jesus chose to live his own life, according to his calling. As a Jew he must have held family life in high regard. Yet a time came when he left them and their ideas for his life and their expectations of him in order to embrace his wider 'family'. *Mark 3:31-35*

We too must learn to listen to and obey the prompting of the Spirit within and the voice of our conscience.

Franz Jaegerstaetter was an Austrian villager, a faithful Roman Catholic. After the annexation of his country by Germany and the outbreak of war, Franz was called up to fight for the Germans. He considered Nazism a great evil and so he refused. His family, his priest, even his bishop, all advised him in the strongest terms to comply. He obeyed his inner voice in spite of them all, and was executed. Today he is considered a hero.

Similarly we should not expect members of our family to bend to our expectations.

My husband and I worked for a number of years with a Lutheran pastor in north Germany. He too had been an open opponent of Hitler. He often stressed the great debt he owed his wife, who never once asked him not to follow his conscience for the sake of her and their children. A friend of his, whose wife implored him to be careful and not to endanger his family, committed suicide.

Maybe when we marry and exchange the rings as a sign of being bound together, we should also include in the ceremony a promise to hold lightly to each other and never to hinder each other from following our consciences. What do you think?

Our young people have to free themselves from the inner need to comply. It is a great pity, however, that in a mood of rebellion they often promptly submit themselves to the sometimes much more dictatorial conformity of a peer group.

Elisabeth Kubler-Ross tells a story of a young man, diagnosed with terminal cancer, who was directed to her for counselling. She asked him, as he had only a few months to live, how he would like to spend them. He had no doubt about that; he had always wanted to play the violin in an orchestra but his father considered it too insecure a job, so he became a solicitor. They found him such a post and, so the story goes, years later he was still playing a violin in an orchestra.

We often do not even realise the pressures on us to conform. We are so strongly conditioned that the society's, family's and church's claims become our own. We are well adapted to our culture and don't know it. We think we are free agents but in fact we live out our roles as expected of us.

What about letting go society's idea, say of a 'beautiful' woman? A real 'man'? What constitutes a 'good' life? What is a 'successful' person?

To be free and able freely to choose, we must become aware of the fact of our conditioning, aware of what is going on in us.

> Does living one's own authentic life mean that we always do as we please?
>
> Did Jesus? *Mark 6:30-34*

PRAYER

Write your own 'freedom prayer'.

CONSIDER

Holy Spirit, right divine,
King within my conscience reign;
Be my law, and I shall be
Firmly bound, for ever free.
                    Samuel Longfellow (1819-92)
                    Hymns & Psalms 289 v4

Advent on Self-Examination partly

SESSION 5

LETTING GO LIFE – DENYING ATTITUDES, FEELINGS, THOUGHTS

To a certain extent this study continues the previous one on conditioning, because we learn our attitudes, feelings and ideas.

Need to love our neighbour as ourselves

We will look at two of these feelings which diminish us and our lives – self-contempt and fear.

SELF-CONTEMPT

We learn early in life that we are not good enough. We may even make a virtue of it, calling it, mistakenly, humility. I heard it stated that we know we are not good enough by the age of three. Surely not that early, I thought. Then I remembered a young woman I used to know who frequently called her two year old son, 'Bad boy!' What does a little child feel when hearing that said frequently and in anger?

We have to let go the idea of our worthlessness or 'badness' and take time to think on our goodness: we are uniquely made by our loving God who considered us worthy of the life and suffering and death of his Son, capable of learning and changing and destined for God and for glory.

Because so much of the time we feel bad about ourselves, we crave compensations: constant approval from others, great success to prove to others and ourselves that we are worth something. We shop and consume more than is good for us or the planet; we need to be right and perfect all the time.

Recently I read a biography of Florence Nightingale. What a life of service and achievement! Yet she spent most of it in misery, feeling worthless. For example, because she could not overcome the resistance of officialdom and introduce all the necessary reforms, only some of them, she considered herself an abysmal failure. She was a victim of perfectionism.

SHARE

Do we demonstrate humility or pride when we feel we can never measure up to our own standards?

READ

> *Cast off all these injuries, unquiet and angered and consequently proud humilities; learn to tolerate yourselves patiently . . . practise gentleness towards yourselves as towards others, reproving yourselves without anger, bitterness or spite.*
>
> De Caussade

SHARE

What we need is not self-condemnation but understanding.

    Do you agree?

Share if you can your negative habits of thought, attitudes and feelings.

Be silent for four minutes.

In the stillness of prayer bring all this unhappy negative conditioning to God and surrender it to him.

Read together and meditate on the many wonderful assurances of God's love and approval of us. Here is one:

> *Do not fear, for I have redeemed you;*
> *I have called you by name, you are mine . . .*
> *Because you are precious in my sight,*
> *and honoured, and I love you . . .*
> *Do not be afraid, for I am with you.*
>
> Isaiah 43:1, 4, 5

PRAYER

> *Compassionate and Loving God, take from me the burden of self-hatred, the whisper of loathing that says I am worthless. Fill me with the spirit of forgiveness and grace, that I may deeply accept that I am accepted just as I am, in Jesus Christ, the Beloved of your Heart.*
>
> Jim Cotter,
Through Desert Places

FEAR

Fear is a great enemy of our ability to live an abundant life. Jesus often repeated, 'Do not be afraid.' He usually countered fear with faith and trust in God's goodness.

Why are you afraid? Have you still no faith?   Mark 5:35-43
Take heart, it is I; do not be afraid.   Matt 14:22-31

Our lives are full of fears of all kinds: some caused by big world events – economic, political and ecological. But some people have more immediate reasons to be afraid. Some live in conditions and under regimes which create fear, and it is fear which makes people slaves. A trailer for the film 'The Krays' stated: *'When people are afraid of you, you can do anything.'* All dictators as well as gangsters know that.

Conditions started to change in Poland after Pope John Paul II visited the country for the first time after his election. Everywhere he went he repeated again and again, 'Do not be afraid.' The Solidarity movement started after that visit, a movement of people no longer afraid.

When the Methodist missionary Vernon Stone returned from China, after many years in a prison camp, he told his colleagues: 'Now I know there is nothing I need to fear.'

But one doesn't need to live under a dictatorship to be afraid. Many of us, living tame enough lives in a welfare state, suffer relentless fears of all kinds: we fear we shall fail as providers, parents, husbands/wives, and as Christians. We fear old age: the loneliness, physical suffering and dependence on others it may bring. We fear death.

How can we overcome the fear of the future?

Soon after the Second World War I met a man who had served in the parachute regiment in Burma, one of the worst theatres of war. I asked him how anyone can jump, knowing that at the bottom he may be met by the enemy's fire or torture. He said, after a moment's hesitation, 'You have to accept that your life is over, that this is *it*, then you can do it.'

That is, I think, the secret. We have to let go our own way and accept what may come, *then* we shall be free to live in the present, without worry about the future.

READ *Romans 6:3-11*

> We believe that we have 'died with Christ'. We believe that whatever happens God will be there. There is nothing that can separate us from his love, and therefore we can say with Vernon Stone, there is nothing we need to fear.

READ *Romans 8:14-18, 31-39*

Hymn 63 (*Hymns & Psalms*) 'All my hope on God is founded' may help too.

SHARE

> Have you ever experienced real fear?
>
> How did you cope with it?

PRAYER

> *Lord, here I am sitting with my fear*
> *I do not know how to handle it.*
> *I open myself to your tender healing touch,*
> *I allow you to love me now.*
> Source unknown

> *Fear him, ye saints, and you will then*
> *Have nothing else to fear;*
> *Make you his service your delight,*
> *Your wants shall be his care.*
> Nahum Tate (1652-1715) and
Nicholas Brady (1659-1726)
Hymn 73 v6 (*Hymns & Psalms*)

INTERCESSIONS

For people enslaved by fear,
For people bravely facing tyrannical regimes,
For people bravely facing feelings of failure and inadequacy
For people learning to live trustfully.

SESSION 6

LETTING GO OUR PAST AND OURSELVES

Compare: *Exodus 12:14ff* — You are to keep this day as a day of remembrance . . .

and: *Luke 22:14-23* — Do this in remembrance of Me . . .

with: *Genesis 19:15-26* — . . . but Lot's wife looked back . . .

and: *Luke 9:57-62* — Anyone who starts to plough . . .

Our roots are in the past and we must not sever them if we would live and grow. We must especially keep alive the recollection of all that God has done for us as a source of life, hope and faith. We know that we can rely on God in the future because we have experienced God's dealings with us in the past.

But there is also our collective and personal past which can be life-denying, apt to poison our present, and we must not allow such past experiences to have a stranglehold on us.

It is as we let the past go that we are free to move on to the next stage of our development. This may be made difficult by the unfinished business of our past. We cannot move forward because past unmet needs, unresolved conflict and unhealed wounds make our progress slow and painful, or even impossible.

We must acknowledge that fact and remember that the past is gone and over, and that which disturbs and impedes us is only the memory of a dead event which cannot now be changed anymore. What can be changed, however, is our attitude to it. In order to do that we must face what it is in the past that is holding us.

For example, is it resentment or anger against someone who has hurt us? We need to acknowledge the reality of our feelings and dissolve the painful memory by forgiveness. There is no healing of memories without letting go those who have wronged or hurt us. If you find it especially difficult to forgive one person, that is *the* person you need to forgive most. And you need only to be *willing* to do it, and the Spirit will *accomplish* it.

Corrie ten Boom and her sister spent years in a Nazi concentration camp during the Second World War, as a punishment for harbouring Jews in their home in Holland. Before Corrie's sister died in the camp, she made Corrie promise that if she survived, she would give her life to work for forgiveness and reconciliation with the Germans. Corrie did.

One day, after she had addressed a meeting in Germany, a man came to her and expressed his appreciation of her attitude. As he stretched out his hand to shake hers, she recognised him as one of the most cruel guards in the concentration camp. She froze, unable to grasp his hand, but remembered her promise and offered an urgent prayer for God's help. She made herself grasp the man's hand. She writes that as their hands met, she was filled with love for that man. The Spirit accomplished her forgiveness when she was willing to take the first step.

We shall never be free of the person who has hurt us if we do not set them free by forgiveness.

And that includes ourselves!

Self-criticism and self-condemnation are part of our deepest self. They lock us into the past and cultivate our *guilt*. We must let them go and change our attitude towards ourselves to one of love and acceptance. This attitude opens us to the transforming power of the Holy Spirit working in us.

Only the loved self can be let go. The rejected, hated, and therefore sore self, demands attention like a sore thumb.

SILENCE

Bring to mind the person and situation you find most difficult to let go . . . Stay with the memory.

PRAYER

O God, our Saviour, help me to be willing to forgive . . .
to let her/him go in freedom.
Help me to be willing to forgive myself . . .
Thank you that your Spirit will find a way for it to happen.

READ   *1 John 3:19b-20*   A great antidote to self-condemnation.

Consider together the attitude of Brother Lawrence:

When he had failed in his duty, he simply confessed his fault, saying to God, 'I shall never do otherwise if you leave me to myself; it is you who must hinder my falling and mend what is amiss.' After this he gave himself no further uneasiness.

Sometimes we cannot let go of something in our past which was a legitimate need, before we have tried to satisfy it. For example, we may have to find out and meet at least some of the needs of the ignored, neglected, repressed child in us who has not been allowed its rightful nurture. When we have done, it will stop its demands and let go of us and our life. We will become integrated and free to be ourselves, to be creative, imaginative, free to love life. We can then 'become like little children', able to enter the kingdom of God.

I once saw a badge saying, 'It's never too late to have a happy childhood.' Let us make sure that, whatever our first childhood was like, we give ourselves that happy childhood now: give ourselves love and appreciation, encouragement in what we do and what we hope; allow ourselves to play and dream, laugh heartily and weep, if we need to; create a safe environment for ourselves within ourselves.

SHARE

Does this suggestion make sense to you?

Can you think of any other part of your past that must be satisfied before you let it go? Share with each other if you can.

Is it all right to dwell on the past that was good?

PRAYER

Compassionate Friend, warm the frozen places of my fear,
Irrigate the deserts of my apathy,
Dismantle the wall around my pain and love,
Lift the burdens of my past,
That I may be free to live in the joy of the Risen Christ.

Jim Cotter,
Through Desert Places

If we are to live out of the future kingdom now, we have to abandon, to let go not only our past but ourselves into that future, into the hands of God. Such letting go is like dying to the old in order to receive the renewal of our inner self. If we cling to our life we diminish it until it becomes less worth living.

READ   *John 12:24-25*

Prayer is very humbling, for you have nothing to shield you from the truth as you stand there before God day after day in your naked poverty. But to flee from this humbling experience is useless; we have to live with our own darkness, failure, temptation, confusion and weakness, because it is the only way in which these areas in us can be opened up to the Lord of the wilderness of our own being, and it may be there, in that unlikely place, we shall see the glory of the Lord.

Maria Boulding, The Coming of God

It is in prayer that we can let go of ourselves into the hands of God.

SHARE your experience of such prayer if you wish.

PRAYER Read together slowly one or all of these prayers:

I am no longer my own, but yours. Put me to what you will, rank me with whom you will; put me to doing, put me to suffering; let me be employed for you or laid aside for you, exalted for you or brought low for you; let me be full, let me be empty; let me have all things, let me have nothing; I freely and wholeheartedly yield all things to your pleasure and disposal.

Methodist Covenant Service

* * * *

*Take, Lord,
and receive all my liberty,
my memory, my understanding
and my entire will,
all that I have and possess.*

*You have given all to me,
to you, Lord, I return it.*

*All is yours;
do with it what you will.*

*Give me only your love
and your grace,
that is enough for me.*

Ignatius of Loyola

APPENDIX A

GUIDED MEDITATION ON LETTING GO

Sit comfortably with your back straight but not rigid . . . Observe your breathing . . . do not try to change it. With each breath you draw in life . . . each time you breathe out you expel the waste and impurities of your body . . . each time you breathe in you open yourself to the Holy Spirit . . . Each time you breathe out you let go the tension in your body: let your scalp and your forehead relax . . . let your jaw drop slightly, relaxed . . . let your tongue and your throat and your shoulders relax . . . let your back and your abdomen relax . . . let your pelvis relax . . . Let your arms and hands relax . . . let your breathing be at peace as you relax your legs and feet . . . let all your tension go down through your feet into the ground . . . be still . . .

You cannot let go if you do not relax your mind.

You have to relax your body before you can relax your mind.

In this relaxed position say to yourself, 'I am willing to let go . . . I release all tension . . . I release all fear . . . I release all anger . . . I release all guilt . . . I let go and I am at peace. I am safe in the love of God . . .

I let go the things from my past that hold me back . . . painful memories . . . resentments . . . wrongs not forgiven . . . I let go the wrongs I have done to others . . . name them . . .

I let go the need to carry the burdens of the world on my shoulders . . . I let go the need to dominate others, to make demands on them . . . I let go the need to punish myself for my past shortcomings . . . I let go my hunger for approval, my need to be right all the time . . .

I let go my fear of failure . . . my ambitions and all that holds me bound and fearful . . .

I rest in the presence of the love of God . . .

I bask in God's tender forgiving, upholding love.

APPENDIX B

GUIDED MEDITATION ON LOSS

Sit comfortably . . . relax . . . be still . . . (as in meditation A).

Come to Christ on his cross . . . the man of losses . . . look at him in his suffering . . .

He had to let go so much: his possessions and home . . . his family . . . his place in village society . . . his prestige . . . his reputation (glutton, friend of sinners) . . . his friends who fled or denied him . . . his power . . . his freedom . . . his dignity (stripped and hung on a tree) . . . his life . . .

Let your feeling surface . . . whatever it is: sorrow . . . pain . . . revulsion . . . compassion . . . anger . . . whatever you feel as you look at Christ in his final loss . . .

Get in touch with your own loss . . . feel it . . . stay with it . . . Is it what life has taken? . . . Is it what you have missed in life? Name your loss . . . stay with it . . . return to Christ on the cross . . . let him look at your loss . . . share your loss with him . . . He shares in whatever hurts and grieves you . . . speak to him of your loss and hurt . . . listen to him . . . stay with him for a while . . . united by suffering and loss . . .

If you can, place your loss there, at the foot of his cross . . . receive his love and blessing . . . give him all of your love . . . open yourself to his healing . . . take time over it . . . stay with him as long as you wish, now and in the silence to follow . . .

Repeat this meditation at home if you wish.

APPENDIX C

GUIDED MEDITATION ON THE PAST

Sit comfortably, relax, let your breathing quieten . . . (as in Meditation A)

Bring your sin to Christ crucified . . . all the ways in which you have missed the mark . . . in which you have fallen short of the glory . . . all the times when you put your own glorification before the glory of God . . . name them, one by one . . .

Jesus bore them all on the cross . . . they have been taken away . . . they are forgiven . . . your relationship of love and trust with God has been restored . . . receive that loving relationship . . . your guilt has been removed . . . do not cling to it, let it go . . .

It belongs to the past . . . receive your freedom, freedom of the child of God . . . freedom to be yourself . . . freedom to start again, today . . . to live *now* . . . The past has no power over you . . . Jesus has healed your wounds as he suffered his . . . let go your hurts, your pain, your memories of the past . . . let the wounds of Christ be your healing . . . If you have regrets about doing harm to someone else, bring that harm, bring their wound to Christ . . . Pray his healing on them . . . Your wronged friend is safe in the life of Christ . . . God can use his/her experience of being harmed for their making . . . God is at work turning their suffering into growth . . .

Now that you have left all your past in God's keeping, take new life from him who said, 'I have come that they may have life, life in all its fullness' . . . Stay with this gift for as long as you wish, now or later at home.

BOOKLIST

If you want to follow up some of the thoughts and issues of this study, the books listed here may be of use. They have been an inspiration and a help to me.

AUTHOR	TITLE	PUBL.	COMMENTS
Jim Cotter	Through Desert Places By Stony Paths	Cairns Pub.	Contemporary reworking of the Psalms
Anthony de Mello	Sadhana	Image	Guided Meditations
Anthony de Mello	Awareness	Fount	
Francis Dewar	Living for a Change	DLT	On our gifts
Peter Harvey	The Morals of Jesus		The hard sayings of Jesus
Gerard Hughes	God of Surprises	DLT	Finding Christ in our depths
Albert Nolan	Jesus before Christianity	DLT	Getting to know Jesus
Henri Nouwen	In the House of the Lord	DLT	From fear to love
Henri Nouwen	In the Name of Jesus	DLT	Christian leadership
John V Taylor	A Matter of Life and Death	SCM Press	Coming alive
John V Taylor	Kingdom Come	SCM Press	
Stephen Verney	The Dance of Love	Fount	The love of God and our love

Jim Cotter's books can be obtained direct from Cairns Publications, 47 Firth Park Avenue, Sheffield, S5 6HF.

GUIDELINES FOR GROUP LEADERS

(Based on ten points for leaders by Ivor Smith-Cameron)

1. Most groups are more fruitful if their size does not exceed twelve members.

2. A circle is the best arrangement for seating as everyone can see one another. Latecomers should not be allowed to sit outside the circle as that makes participation difficult, and remaining a stranger easy.

3. All conversation in a group belongs to the group. Private remarks should be discouraged. The members should be encouraged to talk about themselves and their experiences and to reflect on them. By talking in a vague general way, the group can 'slither off' uncomfortable and disturbing matters which, properly discussed, could help to transform and change lives.

4. The leader will need to be highly sensitive to the needs of the members. Some of us have too much to say; some have too little. Some have an axe to grind, a matter which they raise at every opportunity regardless of its relevance. Some say what they think is suitable, rather than what they really believe. It is important for the leader to handle these matters sensitively yet boldly, encouraging the silent, but not being afraid to check those who over-contribute; to be able to handle conflict without stifling it, and to encourage the confrontation of unpalatable truths.

   The leader must not be frightened of long periods of silence. Carefully used, such periods of silence can be most creative.

5. It is important that all group members should be equally valued. Everybody has a contribution to make. We need to create a climate in which members can face and evaluate the importance of their own experiences, and in which such experiences can be shared. It is most important for the leader to encourage such sharing and to help to interpret the experience. It needs to be done with sensitivity and respect for the one who shares.

6. The leader needs to come to the meeting prepared to lead, having read and thought on the subject of the day. If she/he has considered the questions, not in order to produce the answer for the group, but to understand the feeling and reactions they may evoke, so much the better.

7. Ongoing intercessory prayer for the group members is a very important area of preparation because it enables the leader to be open to the Spirit, and also to the needs and opportunities which the life of the group brings with it for those concerned.

8. If a climate of relaxed preparedness is to be achieved, the leader needs to be ready before the meeting time to welcome the participants. It is helpful if the room is warm and tidy and reasonably comfortable. A cup of tea or coffee is also not without meaning for preparing the atmosphere.

9. Leaders must be prepared that their attitudes, opinions and values may have to be reappraised. They should avoid ever pressing their views on the group. Too often they are accepted without question and there is a grave loss.

10. It would be helpful if the leaders read one of the books suggested in the book list at the end of the Study. Dewar's *Living for a Change* or Hughes' *God of Surprises* would be a good choice for the leader's preparation.

ACKNOWLEDGEMENTS

The following copyright material has been used by kind permission of the publishers:

Page

4	J Neville Ward, *Friday Afternoon,* Epworth Press.
10	Matthew Fox, *Meditations with Meister Eckhart,* Copyright 1983, Bear & Co, Inc, PO Box 2860, Santa Fe, NM87504.
11, 19, 24	Jim Cotter, *Through Desert Places,* Cairns Publications.
25	Maria Boulding, *The Coming of God,* SPCK, 1994 (reissued).
25	Methodist Covenant Service, 1975 Methodist Conference Office.